7-13-05

FIGHTING FORCES IN THE AIR

A-10
THUNDERBOLT II

LYNN STONE

Rourke
Publishing LLC
Vero Beach, Florida 32964

www.rourkepublishing.com

PHOTO CREDITS: All photos courtesy of the U.S. Air Force

Title page: *An A-10 takes off for a mission into Iraq in March, 2003.*

Editor: Frank Sloan

Library of Congress Cataloging-in-Publication Data

Stone, Lynn M.
 A-10 Thunderbolt II / Lynn M. Stone.
    p. cm. -- (Fighting forces in the air)
 Includes bibliographical references and index.
 ISBN 1-59515-178-8 (hardcover)
 1. A-10 (Jet attack plane) I. Title. III. Series: Stone, Lynn M. Fighting forces in the air.
 UG1242.A28S76 2004
 623.74'63--dc22
                                    2004011741

Printed in the USA

CG/CG

TABLE OF
CONTENTS

THUNDERBOLT II
A-10 AND OA-10

The A-10 Thunderbolt II—better known as the Warthog—is a unique jet aircraft. It is the first U.S. Air Force airplane designed for close combat support of ground forces, day or night. A-10s are often sent into combat zones against targets that friendly ground forces are also fighting. The A-10 carries a massive amount and variety of weapons to complete its main task. The "A" in A-10 stands for attack, and the A-10 carries out attack missions with deadly results.

▲ *A pair of A-10s fly side by side as they return to an air base.*

▲

An A-10 takes off on a mission to support NATO ground forces in Yugoslavia.

The A-10 has other jobs, too. It can help with search-and-rescue missions. It can work closely with **Special Forces**, and it can be an airborne air controller. In an air controller role, an A-10—designated an OA-10—flies over a battlefield or potential battlefield and relays information to other friendly aircraft.

Because it flies at low altitudes and at relatively slow speeds, the A-10 opens itself up to weapon fire from enemy ground positions.

FACT FILE ★

THE A-10'S LOW-SPEED, LOW-LEVEL, HIGH-RISK FIGHTING HELPED EARN IT THE WARTHOG NICKNAME.

A-10 Characteristics

FUNCTION: CLOSE AIR SUPPORT
ATTACK AIRCRAFT

BUILDER: FAIRCHILD REPUBLIC
COMPANY

POWER SOURCE: TWO GENERAL
ELECTRIC TF34-GE-100
TURBOFAN ENGINES

THRUST: 9,065 POUNDS
EACH ENGINE

LENGTH: 53 FEET, 4 INCHES
(16.2 METERS)

HEIGHT: 14 FEET, 8 INCHES
(4.4 METERS)

WINGSPAN: 57 FEET, 6 INCHES
(17.4 METERS)

SPEED: 420 MILES PER HOUR
(672 KILOMETERS PER HOUR)

CEILING: 45,000 FEET
(13,636 METERS)

MAXIMUM TAKEOFF WEIGHT:
51,000 POUNDS
(22,950 KILOGRAMS)

RANGE: 800 MILES
(1,280 KILOMETERS)

CREW: ONE

DATE DEPLOYED: MARCH, 1976

The A-10 can be used against tanks and other armored vehicles, enemy soldiers, gun **batteries**, trucks, radar sites, buildings, and other targets. With a combination of low speed and high **maneuverability**, A-10s unleash their weapons accurately and with great destruction. A-10s often fly combat missions below 1,000 feet (305 m). They can make extremely tight turns in flight and make repeated passes over a target. The Air Force calls this a high "loiter time," because the Warthog can "hang around."

◀

Thunderbolt IIs drop away from a refueling air tanker during a NATO combat mission.

Another plus for the Warthog is that it can take off and land in short distances. The Hog doesn't need a high-class runway. It can fly from a temporary airstrip near front-line fighting. The Warthog is easy to service, too.

For night missions, Warthog pilots wear night goggles. The special goggles and the airplane's Night Vision Imaging System (NVIS) bring objects from the darkness outside into identifiable forms. The airplane's large bubble-top **canopy** also helps with visibility, day or night.

▲ *An A-10 banks into a turn.*

▲ *Landing gear down, an A-10 makes a quick, short-distance landing.*

In a world where the military's fighting aircraft are typically sleek and fast, the A-10 stands out. Although it looks nothing like a warthog, it is not sleek. Its wings are swept back just slightly, and its twin engines stand well above its main **airframe**. It won't be mistaken for an F-15 Eagle or a **stealth** jet.

The A-10 is not fast, and it's not intended to be. If the A-10 were too swift, it could not carry out its attack-and-rescue roles nearly as well. An A-10's listed top speed is 420 miles per hour (672 km/h), well below the speed of sound—about 600 miles per hour (966 km/h) at sea level. The Thunderbolt II's namesake, the original P-47 Thunderbolt fighter of World War II, traveled at about 350 miles per hour (560 km/h) at low altitudes.

▲ *The Thunderbolt II's namesake was the P-47 Thunderbolt fighter plane of World War II fame.*

▲ An A-10 pilot gives the thumbs-up sign from his armored cockpit.

CHAPTER TWO

FLYING THE A-10

An A-10 pilot's flying machine is loaded with safety features, modern **avionics**, and **munitions**. One safety feature is the stronger-than-steel titanium "bathtub" around the pilot position. The armor also helps protect the flight-control system. The airframe is built to survive direct hits from most kinds of bullets and shells, as is the bulletproof canopy. The Warthog's fuel tanks are protected by foam and self-sealing materials to lessen the chance of fire.

▲ *This Warthog landed safely after its starboard engine was damaged by an Iraqi missile.*

The Warthog's flight controls have back-up systems. If the original and back-up **hydraulic** flight control systems are lost, a pilot can still fly the plane manually. The Warthog's low-set wings are designed to keep it airborne even if half a wing has been shot off. A pilot can easily fly a Warthog on one engine.

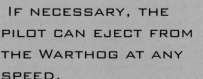

FACT FILE ★

IF NECESSARY, THE PILOT CAN EJECT FROM THE WARTHOG AT ANY SPEED.

The Warthog's avionics are its electronic flight systems. As avionics technology improves, the avionics of the Warthog, like other planes, change. The Warthog's airframe hasn't changed since the first one was delivered to the Air Force in 1975. But its avionics have changed considerably.

▲ *The Warthog canopy covers a cockpit full of modern avionics.*

▲ *Weapons attached to its wings, an A-10 rolls in to mark a target.*

A-10 avionics today include systems for communication, navigation, fire control, and weapons delivery. Heads-up displays (HUDs) in the cockpit indicate airspeed, altitude, dive angle, navigation information, and information about aiming weapons. The pilot can read the HUD without having to look down.

To avoid surface-to-air missiles, the Warthog has **infrared** and electronic defenses. A-10s began to have Global Positioning Systems (GPS) installed in the early 2000s. GPS signals from satellites tell a pilot the plane's exact position.

▲ An airman inspects the Gatling gun of an A-10 based in Korea.

FIREPOWER

The Warthog is something of a flying ammunition dump—except that it fires ammunition as well as stores it. The A-10 can fire weapons, turn, and return to the same target seven seconds later. To enemy defenders on the ground, the growling A-10 is a fire-breathing dragon come to life.

A primary weapon is a 30mm GAU-8/A Gatling Avenger seven-barrel cannon mounted in the Warthog's nose. By continuing rotating barrels and firing in short bursts, none of the gun barrels becomes overheated.

> **FACT FILE**
>
> THE CANNON CAN FIRE UP TO 4,200 ROUNDS PER MINUTE. ITS ARMOR-PIERCING BULLETS CAN STOP BATTLE TANKS.

Loaded with weapons, a Warthog peels into a dive.

The Warthog can carry up to 16,000 pounds (7,200 kg) of mixed weaponry under its wings and main airframe. Among the weapons may be standard bombs, cluster bombs, laser-guided bombs, anti-mine munitions, 2.75-inch (7-cm) rockets, AIM-9 Sidewinder missiles, and AGM-65 Maverick missiles.

Sidewinder missiles are equipped with infrared sensors that follow the heat of an enemy plane's exhaust. The missile explodes when it strikes the target. Mavericks are air-to-surface weapons used to destroy targets such as radar sites and ships.

For their own defense, Warthogs are armed with flares, radar-jamming units, and chaff. Chaff consists of metal strips. When released into the air, chaff can send a false **radar imprint** to enemy radar detectors.

▲ *The needlepoint tip of an air-to-air missile shows on the wing of this Warthog.*

▲ *The Warthog answered the need for a specialized ground-support aircraft.*

COMING OF AGE

The idea for a heavily armored, ground-support aircraft was raised in 1967, during the Vietnam War. The U.S. military needed an airplane that could quickly be called in to support ground forces and destroy enemy strongholds. It also needed an airplane that could destroy Soviet tanks if Europe became a battlefield.

In 1973 the U.S. Air Force chose for production a plane designed by the Republic Aviation Division of Fairchild-Hiller. The first A-10s were battle-ready by October, 1977. Production of the A-10 ended in 1984, 12 years after the first test model had been produced. During that time, the company built more than 700 A-10s.

FACT FILE ★

MORE THAN 350 A-10s REMAIN IN MILITARY SERVICE.

The Vietnam War had ended by the time A-10s were available, and the Soviet Union collapsed in 1991. But Warthogs have been sent into several conflicts. In the Gulf War (1991), A-10s were exceptionally reliable. They almost never missed flights because of a need for repairs. They flew 8,100 **sorties** and launched 90 percent of the Maverick missiles in that conflict. Warthogs accounted for the destruction of 987 tanks, 926 artillery pieces, more than 1,100 trucks, 96 radar sites, and numerous other targets.

◄

Several of the more than 350 A-10s in service are lined up in "Warthog Row" in southern Iraq.

A-10s were used in the United Nations-led operation against Yugoslavia in the spring of 1999. They were **deployed** in Afghanistan in 2002 during the ongoing Operation Enduring Freedom. Sixty A-10s were sent to participate in Operation Iraqi Freedom in 2003.

▲ *An A-10 roars in to attack a target in Iraq during Operation Ivy Cyclone.*

FLYING INTO THE FUTURE

Upgrading military aircraft with the latest avionics and technology is very expensive. How long the Air Force will continue to upgrade the Warthog is unknown. The Air Force budget will have much to do with that.

▲ *An A-10 flies on a NATO combat mission over Europe.*

▲ *These A-10s are equipped with advanced LITENING systems for precision delivery of laser-guided weapons.*

Several new systems have been proposed for the Warthog. Among them are new cockpit displays, airframe changes, and a targeting unit for precision-guided weapons. It's possible A-10 engines will be replaced by upgraded units. The A-10 may continue active service until the mid or late 2020s.

Glossary

airframe (AIR FRAYM) — the wings and shell, or body, of an airplane without its engines or weapons

avionics (AY vee ON iks) — the electronic systems and devices used in aviation

batteries (BAT uh reez) — an army group with artillery guns

canopy (KAN uh pee) — the enclosure over a pilot and airplane cockpit

deployed (dih PLOYD) — to have been placed into a chosen position for possible military use

hydraulic (hi DRO lik) — a system that operates by using water or other liquid

infrared (IN fruh RED) — (also known as *thermal radiation* or *infrared rays*) the invisible-to-the-naked-eye energy rays given off by any warm object, such as a human being, battle tank, or airplane; invisible heat rays that can be detected by special instruments

maneuverability (muh NYUV uh ruh BIL uh tee) — the ability to make changes in direction and position for a specific purpose

munitions (myu NISH unz) — ammunition

radar imprint (RAY DAR IM PRINT) — the image that a flying object leaves on a radar screen

sorties (SORT eez) — missions by one plane

Special Forces — small units of specially trained U.S. soldiers, airmen, sailors, and Marines used for military operations requiring a small, secretive, highly trained force, such as the U.S. Navy SEALs

stealth (STELTH) — the technology and various strategies used to make an aircraft invisible to radar detection

INDEX

FURTHER READING

Green, Gladys and Michael. *Close Air Support Fighters: A-10 Thunderbolt II*. Capstone, 2003

Maynard, Christopher. *Aircraft: The Need for Speed*. Lerner, 1999

WEBSITES TO VISIT

http://www.fas.org/man/dod-101/sys/ac/a-10.htm
http://www.af.mil/factsheets

ABOUT THE AUTHOR

Lynn M. Stone is the author of more than 400 children's books. He is a talented natural history photographer as well. Lynn, a former teacher, travels worldwide to photograph wildlife in its natural habitat.